LONG-AGO STORIES

of the

EASTERN CHEROKEE

LONG-AGO
STORIES
of the
EASTERN
CHEROKEE

LLOYD ARNEACH

Charleston · London

History
PRESS

Published by The History Press
Charleston, SC 29403
www.historypress.net

Copyright © 2008 by Lloyd Arneach
All rights reserved

Illustrations by Elizabeth Ellison.

First published 2008

Manufactured in the United Kingdom

ISBN 978.1.59629.031.0

Library of Congress Cataloging-in-Publication Data

Arneach, Lloyd.
Long-ago stories of the eastern Cherokee / Lloyd Arneach.
p. cm.
ISBN 978-1-59629-031-0 (alk. paper)
1. Cherokee Indians--Folklore. I. Title.
E99.C5A874 2008
398.2089'97557--dc22
2007050746

CONTENTS

HOW THE BEAR
LOST HIS TAIL

This story took place long ago. In those days, the
Bear had a long, bushy tail, and this story tells what
happened to his tail.

The Bear woke up in the middle of the winter.
He came out of his den and began looking around
for food. Everything was covered with snow, and he
started walking through the forest. He saw Brother
Fox coming through the forest toward him.

Brother Fox had a big stringer of fish hanging over
his shoulder. He looked up and saw the Bear coming
toward him, but it was too late for him to run away
with his fish. He didn't want to tell Brother Bear he
had stolen his fish from the Mink, because then the

Bear would take them away from him. So Brother Fox came up with an idea about how he could trick the Bear.

The Bear continued walking along the trail and approached Brother Fox. The Bear said, "That's a lot of fish you've got there. Could you give me one of those fish? I'm awfully hungry."

The Fox knew that he couldn't give the Bear one fish, because then he would want another and another and another. So Brother Fox said, "Bear, I'll tell you how I caught all of these fish and you can catch more fish than I've got here."

And the Bear said, "How did you catch all of those fish?"

The Fox replied, "I went down to the river and I used a rock to knock a hole in the ice. I turned around and stuck my tail down in that hole. The fish started biting the hairs on my tail and it hurt, but that meant more and more fish were biting my tail. I kept waiting and waiting until finally I stood up and I had all of these fish hanging on my tail. Your tail is much bigger than mine and you will catch more fish than I did."

The Bear went down to the river. He found a big rock and used it to knock a hole in the ice. Then he turned around and stuck his long, bushy tail down in the hole. It wasn't long before his tail started to hurt. He thought of all the fish that were biting his tail. Finally, the pain was so strong that he couldn't stand it any longer. The Bear tried to stand up, but he couldn't because the ice had frozen around his tail. He kept straining to stand until finally he gave one last push with his hind legs and pulled free. But he left his long, bushy tail frozen in the ice and all he had left was a short stub of a tail.

And that is why, whenever the Fox sees the Bear in the forest, the Fox runs away—because the Bear still remembers how the Fox caused him to lose his long, bushy tail.

The Bear Man

A Man was hunting in the woods when he saw a Black Bear. He followed the Bear until he was able to shoot it with an arrow. The Bear kept moving. The Man followed and shot the Bear again and again. The Bear did not drop. This was a medicine Bear and it could talk and read the thoughts of people.

The Bear stopped and pulled the arrows from its side. He told the Hunter, "Your arrows will not kill me." He said, "Come to my house and we will live together."

The Hunter thought, "He wants to kill me."

The Bear read his thoughts and said, "I will not harm you."

The Hunter then asked, "How will I get food?"

The Bear replied, "There will be plenty of food."

Finally, the Hunter decided to go with the Bear.

They came to a cave in the mountain. The Bear said, "They are having a council inside. We will see what they decide to do."

They went into the cave and it widened as they went deeper. They saw all kinds of Bears: white, black, brown, young and old. The chief was a great white Bear. The Hunter and the Bear sat in a corner, but the Bears could smell the Hunter.

They asked, "What is that bad smell?"

The Bear chief said, "It is only a stranger come to visit us. Don't talk like that."

It was getting hard to find food in the mountains, and they had sent Bears out to find food. Two Bears came back and said they had found an area in the lowlands where the chestnuts and acorns were knee-deep. They were happy that they would not starve and got ready to dance.

The leader of the Bears was one the Cherokee called "Long Hams." He was a big Black Bear that was always lean. After the dance, the Bears noticed the Hunter's bow and arrows. One said, "This is what Man kills us with. Let us learn how to use them and we can use them against him."

They took the bow and arrows from the Hunter. A Bear put the arrow on the bow and drew the string back. The string got caught in his long claws and the arrow fell to the ground. The Bears realized they could not use the bow and arrows, so they gave them back to the Hunter. The dance and council were now over and everybody left.

The Hunter and the Bear were the last to leave. They traveled on until they came to another cave. The Bear said, "This is where I live."

He went inside the cave. The Hunter followed him. The Hunter was very hungry and he thought, "How will I get something to eat?"

The Bear read his thoughts and sat on his hind legs. He rubbed his stomach with his forepaws and when he opened his paws they were filled with chestnuts. He gave them to the Hunter. He rubbed his stomach with his forepaws again and when he opened his paws they were filled with huckleberries. He gave these to the Hunter. He rubbed his stomach with his forepaws again. When he opened his paws they were filled with blackberries. He gave them to the Hunter. He rubbed his stomach with his forepaws again and when he opened his paws they were filled with acorns. The Hunter said he had had enough.

The Hunter lived with the Bear in the cave all winter long. The Hunter started growing long hair all over his body. He started acting like a Bear, but he still looked like a Man. In early spring, the Bear told the Hunter, "Your people are getting ready for a great hunt. Soon, they will come to find us. They will kill me and take these clothes from me"—he meant his skin—"but they will not harm you. They will take you back with them."

A few days later the Bear said, "This is the day they will come to kill me. The Split-noses will come first to find me." Split-noses are what the Bears called Dogs in those days.

The Bear continued, "They will kill me and drag me outside the cave. They will take off my clothes and then cut me into many pieces. You must cover the blood with leaves. They will take you away. When you have traveled a little ways, look back and you will see something."

Soon, they heard the Dogs coming up the mountain. The Dogs came to the front of the cave and stood barking into the cave. The Hunters looked into the cave and saw the Bear. They shot several arrows into the Bear and he dropped to the ground. They went into the cave and pulled the Bear out. The Dogs were still barking into the cave. The

Hunters looked into the cave again and saw the Man. They started to release their arrows again, but they realized it was a Man and not a Bear. They brought him out of the cave. As the Man was standing outside the cave, the Hunters started skinning the Bear. Then they cut the Bear up into quarters so they could carry him away. When they had finished, they picked up the quarters and the skin and started down the mountain.

The Man covered the blood with leaves and started after the Hunters. After they had gone a little ways, the Man looked back and saw the Bear rise from the leaves, shake them off and disappear into the woods.

When they got close to their village the Man told the Hunters, "They had to put him where nobody could see him and he had to fast and take no water for seven days and seven nights. He had to do this so the Bear's nature would leave him and he could live like a Man again."

They put him in a house and closed it off. The Man's wife found out and came to take him home. They refused to let her see him. She came back every morning and every afternoon, begging and pleading with them to let her take her husband home. Finally, after several days, they let her take him with her. A short time later, the Man died.

If he had remained closed up and had fasted for the entire seven days, he would have been rid of the Bear spirit and would have been able to live as a Man again.

THE HUMMINGBIRD
AND THE CRANE RACE

There once was a beautiful woman with whom both the Crane and the Hummingbird were in love. The Hummingbird was good-looking, and the woman liked the Hummingbird. The Crane was big and awkward, and he was always coming around to see her. She wasn't interested in the Crane, but she couldn't persuade him to stay away. Finally she said to the Crane, "You race the Hummingbird and I will marry whoever wins."

The Crane agreed and so did the Hummingbird.

The woman thought the Hummingbird would win because he was so fast. She did not know that the Crane could fly all night long. They had agreed to start at her house and then fly around the world;

whichever one returned to the house first would get to marry her.

The race began. The Hummingbird darted off, and he was gone like a flash of light. The Crane was slowly flapping along behind him. The Hummingbird flew all day and when evening came the Hummingbird was far ahead. He flew down to a tree limb to sleep for the night. But the Crane flew all night long and passed the Hummingbird a little after midnight. The next morning he came to a stream and stopped to have breakfast.

The Hummingbird woke up that morning and started flying, thinking how easily he was going to win the race. He passed the Crane while he was having breakfast. He didn't understand how the Crane had managed to get ahead of him. But he flew hard, and soon the Crane was far behind him again. The Crane finished eating and started flying. He flew all day and into the night, and this time he passed the Hummingbird before midnight. Each night the Crane passed the Hummingbird earlier and earlier, and it took the Hummingbird longer and longer to catch up to Crane.

On the sixth day it was the middle of the afternoon before the Hummingbird finally caught up to Crane. On the seventh day, the Crane was a short distance from the woman's house when he stopped by a stream for breakfast. After eating, he fixed himself up and flew on to the woman's house. He arrived midmorning. The Hummingbird finally arrived late in the afternoon. Crane had won the race!

The woman declared that she would never have such an ugly fellow as the Crane for her husband—so she stayed single.

CREATION STORY

In the beginning, all of the Animals lived in the sky above the great sky vault. There were so many of them that it was getting crowded. They looked below at the water-covered earth.

They sent down the little Water Beetle. She swam around on the surface for a while and then took a deep breath. She dove deep, down to the bottom, gathered mud in her front legs and started swimming up toward the surface. Soon she was close to the surface, but she was running out of breath. Just below the surface she released the mud and desperately swam upward with all of her legs. When she reached the surface and lay on her back, gasping for air, she

realized that she had dropped the mud. She looked around and she saw that the mud was floating on the water's surface and was growing larger. She went back into the sky.

As the Animals watched from above, they saw the mud grow larger and larger. Finally, it stopped growing, and now the Animals waited for it to dry. They sent down different Birds. Each would fly over the mud trying to find a dry area on which to land. The mud was still wet, and they all came back to wait.

Finally, the great-grandfather of all the Buzzards we know today was sent down. He flew over the land for so long that he was getting tired. He was flying lower and lower until, when he came to Cherokee country, his wingtips touched the ground and made valleys. Mud got on his wingtips, and when he raised them the mud would fly off and form mountains. The other Animals thought that all of the earth would now be mountains and valleys, so they called the Buzzard back. But, to this day, Cherokee country is made up of mountains and valleys.

It was cold and dark in the beginning, so the Conjurers set the sun in the sky. But they set the sun too low and it burned the shell of the Crawfish red. They set it higher and higher until finally it was at the right height. The Cherokee say that the sun is at its highest level at noon. They call this level "seven hands high" or the "seventh level."

HOW THE DEER
GOT HIS ANTLERS

In the beginning, the Animals could talk with one another. In those days, the Deer didn't have the antlers that he has today, and this story tells how the Deer got his antlers.

One day the Deer and the Rabbit got into a tremendous argument. The Rabbit said, "I run so fast even I don't know where I'm going to end up."

The Deer responded, "I can leap a great distance in a single bound."

The Rabbit said, "While you are up in the air, I'll run underneath you and I'll get there before you come down." And they continued to argue back and forth.

The other Animals got tired of listening to them argue all the time. Finally, one of them said, "Why don't you have a race? Whoever wins the race we will know is the fastest Animal of all."

The Deer immediately agreed, but the Rabbit said, "I don't run for nothing. It's got to be worth my time!"

One of the Animals had made a beautiful set of antlers, and he said, "I will give this set of antlers to whoever wins the race."

The Deer looked at the set of antlers and thought how they would look on his head and he said, "Yes, I will run for the antlers."

The Rabbit looked at the antlers and he thought how they would look on his head and he said, "Yes! I will run for the antlers." Then he asked, "Where shall we run?"

One Animal suggested, "Why don't you start here?" He drew a mark on the ground and then he said, "You can run through that thicket over there."

Once again, the Deer immediately agreed. But the Rabbit was a little slow. He said, "Well, I am new to this area. Can I go into the thicket and look around?"

The other Animals said, "Sure, go ahead."

So, the Rabbit went into the thicket and he was gone for a while. The Animals waited and waited.

Finally, they sent a little Animal into the thicket after the Rabbit.

In a few minutes the little Animal came out of the thicket and said, "The Rabbit is cutting a shortcut through the thicket. He's going to cheat!"

The other Animals couldn't believe the Rabbit would cheat in something this important. But in a few minutes, the Rabbit came out of the thicket. He lined up on the mark and told the Deer, "If you don't get up here the antlers are going to be mine."

One of the Animals said, "Rabbit, one of us said you're cutting a shortcut through the thicket and that you're going to cheat!"

And the Rabbit said, "No! No! I'm not!"

And another Animal said, "Rabbit, one of you is lying. We will all go into the thicket to find out who is lying."

All of the Animals went into the thicket. Sure enough, they saw where the Rabbit had been cutting a shortcut through the thicket. They all came back out of the thicket. The Rabbit was quiet—he had been caught in his lie.

Finally, one of the Animals said, "Rabbit, you would cheat and you would lie to win these antlers. Whoever wears these antlers must wear them with honor and respect. Rabbit, you could not wear them with honor and respect. So, we will give them to the Deer."

They called the Deer forward and put the antlers on his head. They grew into his head instantly, and they have grown there from that day until this. But the Deer loses his antlers once a year to remind him that it was not always so.

THE FIRST FIRE

Long ago it was cold. The Thunders sent down lightning and set fire to a hollow sycamore stump on an island. The Animals knew it was on fire because they could see the smoke coming out of the stump.

All of the Animals wanted to go get the fire. They held a great council and it was finally decided which Animal would go get the fire. The Raven was selected. He flew over the water and landed on the top of the stump. The heat was so great that it scorched all of his feathers black. He was scared, and he returned without the fire.

The Hoot Owl went next. He landed on the stump and, while he was looking down into the stump, a blast of hot air came up and nearly burned out his eyes. He rubbed and rubbed his eyes until they turned red. They are still red to this day.

The Screech Owl and the Horned Owl went next. They flew over and landed on the stump. They were nearly blinded by the smoke and the wind blew ashes up and made white rings around their eyes. They returned without the fire.

The Racer Snake went next. He swam across and found a small hole at the bottom of the stump. He went inside, but there was too much smoke and heat. He darted back and forth over the hot ashes until he finally found the hole and escaped outside. He was burned black and, to this day, he darts back and forth over his trail. Today, he is known as the Black Racer.

A Great Snake tried next. He swam across and climbed up the outside of the stump. When he put his head over and down into the stump, the smoke choked him, and he fell into the stump. Before he could get out again, he was burned as black as the Racer.

This time, the little Water Spider said she would go. She was the one with red hairy legs that was so light she could walk on the water. She wove a basket from her silk and placed it on her back. She crossed the water and went into the stump. She took up a coal, placed it in her bowl and returned with the coal. Ever since then we have had fire, and the little Water Spider has kept her bowl.

THE FIRST STRAWBERRY

Long ago, the First Man and the First Woman appeared on the Earth. They got into a big argument, and the First Woman decided she had had enough of the First Man. So she started walking away as fast as she could go. The First Man thought, "I'll let her go. I don't need her around here anyway."

But then he started thinking, "Well, I enjoyed talking with her, I enjoyed sitting with her and I enjoyed just being around her. Maybe I was wrong."

So the First Man started walking after the First Woman. He walked all day long, and he could see her far ahead of him, a little dot on the distant horizon. The Sun fell. The First Man walked on into the night after the First Woman. He walked all night long, and when the Sun rose the next morning in the east, he looked ahead and could just barely see the First Woman. She, too, had walked all night long, and she was still the same distance ahead of him. He kept walking—he had to catch her and tell her he had been wrong.

As the Sun rose into the sky, he looked down on the First Man and took pity on him. The Sun decided to help the First Man and he caused some huckleberries to grow up along the path the First Woman was taking. The First Woman walked past the huckleberries and didn't pay any attention to them. The Sun tried again, this time making some blackberries grow up along the path she was taking. The First Woman walked past the blackberries and didn't pay any attention to them either. The Sun tried again. He made a new fruit grow up in the field through which she was walking. The First Woman was walking through the fruit, crushing it under her feet and not paying any attention to it, so the Sun added a scent to the fruit. The scent started drifting up until finally it reached the woman's nose.

The First Woman stopped and looked around to see from where that wonderful smell was coming. She looked behind her and saw where she had crushed the fruit. She bent down, picked up one of the fruits and smelled it. That was where the wonderful smell was coming from! She took a small bite and it was delicious. She took another bite and it was wonderful. She ate the rest of it and then she looked around and saw the entire field was filled with this new fruit. She thought, "My husband would enjoy this."

She started gathering the new fruit. When she had finally gathered all that she could carry, she turned and started back to meet her husband. And that was how the First Man and the First Woman came back together again. The First Woman was coming back to share the delicious food with the First Man. Today, this food is red and it is in the shape of a heart because it brought the First Man and First Woman back together again. We know this food as the strawberry.

THE FIRST TOBACCO

In the old days, before the Cherokee lost the gift of being able to talk to the Animals, we had one tobacco plant. In those days, we used it for healing. There was an Old Woman of our people who took sick. The Medicine Man went to see her. After he had examined her, he realized that he could heal her with a leaf from the tobacco plant. He told a Warrior to go get him a leaf. The Warrior went into the forest, but when he got to where the tobacco plant had been, he found a great big hole in the ground. He looked on the ground around the hole and he saw the tracks of Geese.

In those days, Geese were fierce fighters and nobody wanted to fight with them unless they really

had to. The Warrior realized that the Geese had dug up the plant and had taken it to their camp far away in the south. He went back to the Medicine Man and told him what he had found.

The Medicine Man called in the Animals and the Warriors. He told them that the Old Woman was sick and that he could heal her with a leaf from the tobacco plant, but the Geese had taken it to their camp in the south. He then asked for someone to go to their camp and bring back a leaf.

The Deer said he would go. He traveled very fast and after a while he could hear the Geese, for they were as noisy then as they are now. He eased through the bushes until he came to a clearing. The tobacco was planted out in the middle of the clearing and the Geese were in a circle guarding it. The Deer went running out into the clearing, leaped over the Geese and went charging toward the tobacco plant. The Geese gave the alarm call and more Geese flew in from all over. They knocked the Deer to the ground and killed him.

The Medicine Man knew when the Deer had passed. He called the Animals and the Warriors together again. They were told that the Deer would not be coming back and they all knew what that meant. The Medicine Man asked for someone else to go and this time the Bear said he would go. The Bear traveled to the south and after a while he could hear the Geese. Easing through the bushes, he saw the Geese and the tobacco plant. The Bear went charging out into the clearing, knocking the Geese aside. The Geese gave the alarm call and others flew in from all over. They knocked the Bear to the ground and killed him.

The Medicine Man knew when the Bear had passed. He called the Animals and Warriors together again. They were told that the Bear would not be coming back. Again, the Medicine Man asked for someone to go, and this time the Mole said he would go. The Mole traveled underground, coming up to the surface to get his bearings and then returning underground. Finally, he came up to the surface and could hear the Geese. Easing through the bushes, he saw the Geese and the tobacco plant. Going back underground, he started digging toward the tobacco. As noisy as the Geese are, they have very good hearing. They followed the noise of the Mole digging underground, dug him up and killed him.

The Medicine Man knew when the Mole had passed. He called the Animals and Warriors together again. He told them the Mole would not be coming back and asked for someone else to go. This time, everybody was quiet. The Deer, as fast and agile as he was, had been killed. The Bear, as big and formidable as he was, had been killed. The Mole, as small and secretive as he was, had been killed. Finally, the Hummingbird said he would go.

Everybody looked at him and started laughing. Someone asked, "You? What can you do?"

The Hummingbird said, "I will try. Does anyone else want to go?"

Everyone was quiet. The Hummingbird said, "Then I will go."

The Hummingbird was very fast and it wasn't long before he could hear the Geese. He flew up and landed on the branch of a tree. Below him were the circle of Geese and the tobacco plant. Darting over the Geese, he landed on the tobacco plant. Quickly, he looked around and realized the Geese were so busy talking that they hadn't seen him. Snipping off some seeds and a leaf, he held them in his beak. Darting back over the heads of the Geese, he landed on the tree branch again. He still hadn't been seen. After flying north, back to the land of the Cherokee, the Hummingbird went to the Medicine Man and gave him the seeds and the leaf.

The Medicine Man called in the Warriors. He gave each of them a seed and told them, "Go plant these through our land so we will never want for our medicine again."

Then he crumpled up the leaf and burned it. Gently, he fanned the smoke across the Old Woman's face and she was healed. She lived for many more years, sharing her knowledge with our people.

The Hummingbird teaches us the lesson in this story. Too often we will look at this shell that we live in and determine what a person can or cannot do. That is wrong. The Hummingbird teaches us that the shell is not important; what is important is what is in the heart.

ISHI

In northern California, near the small town of Oroville, on August 29, 1911, a rancher was awakened early in the morning by his dogs barking. He got a light and his gun and went out to check on what was causing all the noise. In one of his buildings he found a half-naked man shivering with fright. He called the sheriff. The sheriff took the man to jail and tried to talk to him. The man did not respond. The sheriff sent for one of the elders of a nearby tribe. The elder sat with the man for a while trying to talk. Finally, he came out and told the sheriff, "He speaks an old language. I can't understand him."

By now, newspaper reporters had heard of the capture of a "wild Indian." Their headlines proclaimed, "Last Wild Indian Captured!" People were coming from all over to see the wild Indian. One day a man walked into the sheriff's office and said his name was T. Waterman and he was a professor of anthropology from the University of California. He wondered if he could try and talk to the wild Indian. The sheriff agreed, and led the professor back to the man's cell.

The professor tried several of the California tribal languages that were spoken at that time. The man did not respond to any of them. Finally, in desperation, the professor tried some languages that were extinct. When trying one of the words, he saw the man glance up. The professor tried the word again. The man said the word a different way. The professor said it the same way the man had and he saw the man sit up. He was responding! The professor tried other words and the man started talking. Each time he would say the word a little differently than the professor. The professor realized the man was speaking "Yana," a language that had been extinct for decades.

The professor called his associate at the university and told him the wild Indian was speaking Yana.

Arrangements were quickly made for the wild Indian to become a "ward" of the university. The sheriff agreed since he couldn't talk to the prisoner at all.

The wild Indian was taken to the university where Professors Waterman and Kroeber would sit and talk to him. He was taken to the university teaching hospital, which was next to the museum. There, Dr. Sexton Pope examined him to make sure he was not suffering from any illnesses. After working with him for a while, the professors realized that he was from the Yahi, a part of the southern Yana Indians. By Yahi tradition, he was not allowed to speak his name or the names of the dead. So, Professor Kroeber gave him the name "Ishi," which is Yana for "man." As they learned more of his language, Ishi was also learning English. Soon, Ishi was able to carry on a simple conversation in English. Dr. Pope was very interested in archery and was soon asking Ishi questions about the type of bow and arrows he used. Ishi enjoyed talking about his way of life. Soon they became close friends.

Ishi was fascinated by the "healing place," his word for the hospital. He would roam the halls, making friends and learning. He could not understand how they could "kill" a person, cut him open, close him back up and then he would come back to "life."

As others learned more about Ishi's way of life, their respect for him grew. At first, they didn't understand why Ishi would cringe whenever he heard a dog barking. Ishi explained that barking dogs meant death to his people. His people would hear the dogs barking as they came up the mountains and they would know that the white men were coming with guns to kill them. They would scatter into the mountains. They would hear gunshots and later, when they would gather at the meeting place, there were always some who were missing. Each time, their numbers grew smaller and smaller. Finally, there were only Ishi, his mother and his sister. Once again they heard the dogs and they scattered into the mountains. Ishi had heard gunshots in the direction his mother had taken. Then he heard gunshots in the direction his sister had taken. Later, he returned to the gathering place and waited for several days, but neither his mother nor his sister showed up. He never saw his mother or sister again. Everybody he had ever known was gone.

It was hard work finding food, and it took several people working together to gather enough food to survive. One person by himself could not gather enough food to live. Soon, starvation drove Ishi down out of the mountains. It was then that he was found in the rancher's buildings looking for food.

Ishi would be taken on sightseeing tours to show him the "white man's world." They thought that skyscrapers with people living in them would impress him. He simply said, "Like big mountains. I lived in mountains."

They pointed out airplanes in the sky. Ishi had seen and heard them flying over often enough that he paid them no attention. But he was intrigued with a window shade that would roll up. "Where does it go?" he asked. Then he was taken to the beach. He was stunned! When his people had gathered, he had only seen fifty to sixty people at the most. There on the beach he saw thousands. He did not know that that many people existed in the world.

Bows would disappear from the museum. The museum staff would know that Dr. Pope and Ishi were trying them out and discussing the various merits of each bow. When they were finished, the bows would mysteriously return to their place in the museum.

Ishi was given his own room and was assigned the task of helping out in the museum. He had learned how to wear the clothes of the white man. Soon, he learned how to get around using the trolley cars and was doing his own shopping.

He loved talking about his way of life, and he was asked if he would be willing to talk to the public about it. He agreed, and a Sunday lecture date was sent to the newspapers. He was asked if he would wear his traditional clothing for his talk. He said, "No." With quiet dignity he said it would be very impolite to wear his clothing in the white man's world. When the Sunday of the lecture arrived, several people showed up. They listened intently to Ishi and asked many questions. When it was over, they asked when he would do it again. The response was totally unexpected, but another date was set. This time more people showed up. The word quickly spread, and Ishi's talks were eagerly received. Soon, it was a regular Sunday afternoon event at the museum. By this time more people were coming to hear Ishi on Sunday afternoon than were coming to the museum during the rest of the week.

Then, one day, Ishi was found lying on the floor of the museum. He was rushed to the hospital.

Dr. Pope immediately took charge, arguing that no one knew Ishi better than he did. Word quickly spread throughout the hospital that Ishi was seriously ill. As usual, Ishi had made many friends when he was roaming the "healing place." Members of the staff quietly gathered in the hallway outside of his room awaiting word of his condition. Nurses were scurrying in and out of Ishi's room carrying Dr.

Pope's tests as he tried to find out what was wrong with him. Finally, Dr. Pope came out of Ishi's room. Sweat beaded his forehead and his face was pale. Quietly, he told the waiting staff, "Ishi is in the latter stages of tuberculosis." Ishi had been feeling weak for some time and hadn't been able to keep his food down. But he hadn't said anything because he didn't want to be a "bother" to anyone. On March 25, 1916, Ishi passed away.

As was the custom among his people, the following items were placed in his coffin: his favorite bow and five arrows, several obsidian shards, a pouch of dried corn and a pouch of acorn meal for his journey.

He was then cremated. Ishi's ashes were placed in a small black pueblo jar. The inscription reads, "Ishi, the last Yana, 1916."

Ishi had learned the language, the customs and even how to wear the clothes of a culture that had hunted his people to extinction and yet he was the one called the "savage."

I will end Ishi's story with his own preferred phrase of farewell, "You stay, I go."

THE MAGIC LAKE
OF THE ANIMALS

In western North Carolina, deep in the Great Smoky Mountains, you will find the headwaters of the Oconaluftee River. It is said that if you go west from these headwaters you will find a large, grassy plain. There will be no Animals that you can see, for this is the Magic Lake of the Animals.

To see what is there, first you must fast the day before going to this area. The next morning, after fasting, as you travel to the west you will hear many Ducks and the call of other Animals. Soon you will see flocks of Ducks and Geese flying overhead. If you move quietly through the bushes, you will see a huge, shallow lake. Water will be pouring out of the

cliffs overlooking the lake. Waterfowl of all kinds will be resting on the surface. Animals will be walking around the shore.

An Animal that is injured will wade out into the lake and swim across. When he comes out on the other side he will be healed. If an Animal has been injured and can make it to the lake then he can be healed. The Animals move around the lake in peace. Here, there is no fighting.

This is the Magic Lake of the Animals.

The Milky Way

Long ago, a Cherokee family had ground up some cornmeal and placed it in a basket outside their cabin. The next morning when the Father got up, he went over to the basket. He looked inside, and all of the cornmeal was gone. He did not know what had happened to the cornmeal. He woke up his family. They talked about what had happened.

That day, they ground up some more cornmeal, and that evening they left the cornmeal in the basket outside their cabin once again. But this time, when it grew dark, the Father hid in the bushes around the clearing. He sat down to wait. He waited until long after midnight, when a giant Dog appeared

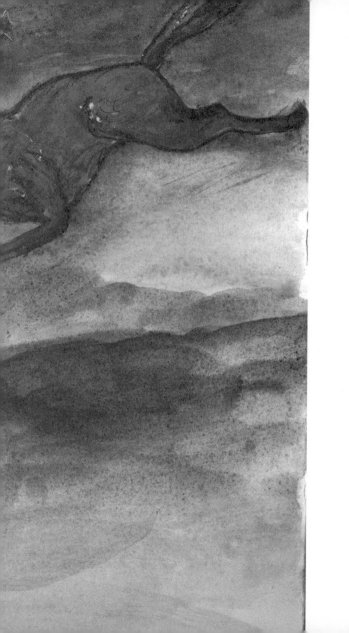

and came down out of the northern sky. The Dog landed on the ground, walked over to the basket of cornmeal and started eating. He stayed there until he had finished all the cornmeal. Then he walked to the bushes and disappeared.

Now the Father knew what had happened to the cornmeal. The next morning he woke up his family, gathered them around him and told them what had happened. They worked on a plan to stop this from happening again. Finally, they came up with a plan they thought would work. They ground up some more cornmeal, put it in the basket and left the basket outside their cabin once again. But this time, when it grew dark, everybody picked up drums or switches and hid themselves in the bushes around the clearing.

They waited and waited, until finally, out of the northern sky, the giant Dog again appeared. He came down out of the sky, landed and walked over to the cornmeal. He started eating. At the Father's signal, everybody jumped out of the bushes. They started yelling at the top of their lungs, beating on the drums or rushing toward the Dog with their switches. They started hitting the Dog with their switches and yelling and drumming. The Dog was so stunned that he whirled around, gave a mighty leap and disappeared back into the northern sky. But because he had been eating cornmeal, cornmeal streamed out of his mouth as he leaped back into the sky. And instead of falling down to the earth, this cornmeal floated up into the sky. Today we know that cornmeal as the Milky Way.

WHY THE MINK SMELLS

Long ago, there was nobody here but the Animals. The Mink was a great thief. He would steal from everybody, and all of the Animals got tired of the Mink stealing all the time. So they decided to teach him a lesson. They built a fire and then grabbed the Mink and threw him into the fire. He would try to escape and the Animals would throw him back. Finally, they saw his coat had turned black and he smelled like roasted meat. They decided the Mink had learned his lesson and pulled him out of the fire. His coat is still black, and whenever he gets excited he smells like roasted meat. But the Mink did not learn his lesson, and he steals to this day.

PLEIADES AND THE PINE

There were seven young Boys who loved to play a game. They would roll a round stone along the ground and throw a curved stick after it trying to strike it. Their Mothers would scold them for playing the game all the time, but it didn't do any good.

One day, all the Mothers gathered up stones and boiled them in the pot for dinner. The Boys came home hungry and their Mothers got the stones out of the pots and said, "Since you like to play better than come home, take the stones for your food."

The Boys were angry. They left the cabins and went down to the townhouse. They began to dance around the townhouse.

At last, the Mothers went looking for the boys because they were afraid something was wrong. They found all of the Boys dancing around the townhouse. They noticed that the Boys were rising off the ground as they danced. Each time around, they rose higher and higher off the ground. The Mothers began jumping up to try and catch the Boys, but most of them were too high to reach. Only one of the Mothers was able to jump up and grab her son by the ankle and pull him down. But she pulled with such force that he struck the ground, sank into it and the ground closed up over him.

The others rose higher in the sky, until finally they were lost forever to the people. We see them now as the Pleiades, which the Cherokee call "The Boys."

The Mother, whose son sank in the ground, came every morning and every afternoon to cry when he disappeared. Her tears were so many that they turned the ground wet, and finally a small sprout appeared out of the ground. This sprout grew taller and taller until it became a tree that we now call the Pine.

WHY THE POSSUM'S TAIL IS BARE

In the old days, the Possum had a long, beautiful tail, and he was always grooming his tail and telling everybody how beautiful his tail was. All the Animals got tired of listening to Possum brag about his tail.

The Animals' council came together, and they decided to have a big dance at which everybody could sing their songs. The Rabbit was the messenger for the Animals' council and he was sent out to tell all the Animals about the dance.

The Rabbit went around to all of the Animals' homes. Finally, he came to the Possum's home. He called to the Possum, and the Possum came out. The Possum was grooming his tail as usual and he asked

the Rabbit, "Don't you think my tail is beautiful today?"

The Rabbit agreed and he said, "Possum we're going to have a great dance, and everybody will be singing their songs and doing their dances."

The Possum said, "You will have a place of honor for me where everybody can see my tail as they dance by."

The Rabbit agreed, and said, "Possum will have a place of honor there in the dance arena. And I brought the Crickets with me to comb and dress the fur on your tail."

Now, the Cherokee know the Crickets are great haircutters, and the Rabbit had given these two Crickets very special instructions.

The Rabbit told the Possum, "They will comb and clean your hair, then wrap it with bark and tie it with vines to keep it clean. And you don't untie the bark and the vines until it's your turn to get up to dance."

The Possum agreed. He walked over to a stump, sat down and the Crickets started working on his tail. The Crickets trimmed the fur next to the bottom of his tail and then they wrapped it with bark and tied it in vines all the way down to the end. Then the Crickets told Possum, "Now don't untie it until it's your turn to get up to dance."

Possum agreed. He went down to the dance area on the appointed day. The Animals were all gathered around waiting to get started. The Possum called, "Rabbit, Rabbit!"

The Rabbit came bounding up to the Possum. The Possum said, "Where is my place of honor?"

The Rabbit replied, "We have rolled a rock right up here, and you can sit on this rock, and everybody will dance in front of you."

The Possum agreed and sat down on the rock and put his tail, still wrapped in the bark with the vines, behind him. They started calling Animals up. Each, in turn, would dance around a circle in front of the Possum and sing his song.

Finally they called for the Possum to dance and sing. The Possum stood up, reached behind him, untied the vines and pulled the bark off his tail. And then he started dancing and singing his song, "I am the only one who has a tail like this."

The Animals yelled, "Ah ha!"

And the Possum thought, "They like my song. This is good."

He sang and danced some more, "I am the only one with a tail like this in the whole world."

And the Animals again yelled, "Ah ha!"

The Possum thought, "This is a very good song."

He sang and danced again, "Don't you wish you had a tail like mine?"

This time the Animals were laughing. Some of them were lying on the ground and pointing at the Possum.

The Possum looked around. He didn't know what they were laughing at. Finally he looked behind him and he saw that all of the hair had been cut off his tail. All that was left was the naked tail that he has to this very day. The Possum was so embarrassed that he fell over in a faint, which is what he does to this very day whenever he is frightened or embarrassed. And now you know the reason why.

The Rabbit Goes Duck Hunting

The Rabbit was always bragging that whatever someone had done, he had done it better. On top of that, he claimed that whatever it was had been harder when Rabbit had done it.

One day, the Mink was talking to some of the Animals and telling them what a great fisherman he was. The Rabbit said he was a great fisherman too. The Mink just looked at him. Then the Mink said, "I'm a great duck hunter too."

"Well, I'm a great duck hunter too," said the Rabbit.

The Mink had had enough of the Rabbit's bragging so he turned to the Rabbit and said, "All

right Rabbit. Why don't you show us what a great duck hunter you are."

The Rabbit said, "All right Mink! But, how can I show you with no ducks around here?"

Then the Mink said, "There's a little pond on up the river where there are always ducks. We can go up there and you can show us all what a great duck hunter you are."

The Rabbit was caught. He didn't have any choice but to go with the Mink. So all the animals went up the riverbank, and soon they came to a pond. The Mink pointed to the ducks across the pond and said, "Rabbit, go show us what a great duck hunter you are."

The Rabbit said, "Mink, go ahead and try it and then I'll show you how it should be done."

The Mink said, "OK," and he slid off the bank into the water. He swam across the pond underwater and the ducks had no idea the Mink was approaching. He swam underneath the ducks and he grabbed one by the legs, jerking it underwater. It happened so fast that the other ducks didn't see him disappear. The Mink swam back under the water, got out on the bank and held up his duck. "I've got mine, now you get yours."

Well, while the Mink had been swimming underwater, the Rabbit had gone to a nearby tree and started stripping the bark off of the tree. He made a lasso out of the bark by weaving it together. By the time the Mink got back, the Rabbit had finished making a rope with a noose on the end of it. When the Mink showed his duck and asked Rabbit to go get his, Rabbit picked the lasso up and held it in his mouth. He walked down into the water and started trying to swim, but it was hard to swim with the bark in his mouth. Water kept getting in his mouth. He was splashing and making a big noise in the water. The ducks turned around to see what was making all the noise. They realized that it was just the Rabbit trying to swim and they didn't pay any more attention to the noise.

The Rabbit started getting the idea of how he should swim, but Rabbits aren't that good as swimmers. The Rabbit started getting a little bit better as he tried going underwater and discovered he had to keep his mouth closed to keep water from getting down his throat. He kept coming up and sputtering, but he was learning fast and finally he was able swim underwater for some distance. He kept getting closer to the ducks and still they were not paying any attention to him.

Finally, the Rabbit got close enough. He took a deep breath and swam along underneath the ducks with the noose in his paw. He came up in the middle of the ducks and threw the noose over the head of one of the ducks. All the ducks went flying wildly into the sky and the Rabbit managed to lasso of one of the biggest ducks in the group. As the ducks started flying off the water, the noose tightened up around the biggest duck's neck and he started to pull the Rabbit out of the water. The Rabbit was hanging on to the rope until he looked down and saw how far below the Earth was. The Rabbit realized he was going to go even higher and he decided to turn the duck loose. He let go of the rope and fell. He fell down into the hollow stump of a sycamore tree.

The Rabbit was stunned for a while and then he was able to get up and move around. He looked around the bottom of the stump for a way out. He didn't see any holes, so he looked higher around the stump and didn't see any holes up high. Then he looked up to the top of the stump and there was a way out. But he couldn't jump that high at a standstill, and there was no room to get a running start. He kept trying and trying to jump out, but he couldn't even get halfway up the stump. He stayed there for long time, and he was starting to get hungry.

Finally, the Rabbit started eating his fur, which is what he does to this very day whenever he is starving.

Then he heard some Children's voices outside. He listened very closely, and knew that the Children were approaching the stump. The Rabbit started singing to them. He sang, "Come closer and see my beautiful fur." The Children started looking around to see where the voice was coming from. They finally realized it was coming from the stump.

They surrounded the stump and said, "Who are you?"

And the Rabbit answered back, "Cut a hole in the stump, so you can see my beautiful fur."

The Children didn't have an axe with them. One of them was sent back to the village to bring an adult with an axe. The Child arrived back at the village, told his Father what they had heard coming from the stump and asked his Father to bring his axe. The Father was interested in this talking stump. He had never heard of anything like this. He picked up his axe and followed his Child into the forest.

When they reached the stump, the Father could hear the Rabbit singing to the Children. The Rabbit was still singing about how beautiful his fur was, and claiming that they should cut a hole in the stump so that they could see his beautiful fur. The Father started using his axe on the stump, cutting a hole in the side. The Rabbit told him to cut the hole larger so they could see all of him. The Father made the hole much bigger. Finally, the Rabbit said, "That's big enough. Now stand back so you can see all of my fur."

They moved away from the stump. The Rabbit jumped out of the stump and ran away into the forest. And that's the story of the Rabbit that went duck hunting.

THE REMOVED
TOWNHOUSES

Long ago, the Cherokee who lived on the Valley and Hiwassee Rivers heard voices in the air warning them of wars and bad things to come. The voices invited them to live with the Immortals under the mountains and waters. For many days the voices could be heard, and then they said, "If you would live with us, gather everyone in your townhouses and fast there for seven days and no one should raise a shout or a war whoop in all that time. Do this and we shall come and you will see us and we shall take you to live with us."

The people were afraid of the bad things to come and they knew that the Immortals of the mountains and the waters were always happy. So they held a council meeting and decided to go with the Immortals. The people of one town came together in their townhouse. They fasted and prayed for six days. On the seventh day they heard a noise from far away in the mountains. It got closer and louder, until all the people could hear was thunder and the ground shook under their feet. They were frightened, and some screamed.

The Nunnehi lifted up the townhouse with its mound to carry it away. They were surprised by the screaming and let some of it drop to the ground. They recovered, and took the rest of the townhouse, with the people in it, to Lone Peak. Today, near the head of the Cheowa River, there is a huge rock. This is the townhouse with the people in it that was changed long ago into solid rock. The people are inside of it, invisible and immortal.

There was another town where the people also prayed and fasted. This was on the Hiwassee River, near where Shooting Creek flows into it. At the end of seven days the Nunnehi took the people down into the waters. It is said that on a summer's day, when the wind blows across the water, if you have good hearing and listen quietly, you can hear the people talking under the water. When the Cherokee fish the deep water in this area, their lines will stop and they know it is their fellow tribesmen who are holding the line and do not want to be forgotten.

At the time of the Removal in 1838, the Cherokee who lived along the Valley and Hiwassee Rivers were especially grief-stricken, for they were also forced to leave their relatives who had gone to the Nunnehi.

SEQUOYAH

A long time ago, the Cherokee saw the white man doing many things that they had never seen before. They would see a white man open up what looked like a leaf. He would look at it and know what another white man far away had said. At first the Cherokee did not know what they were doing. We did not have a word for "letter." The closest thing we had that looked like a letter was a leaf, and because whoever read the leaf knew what someone else far away had said, the "leaf" talked. We called letters "talking leaves."

There was one man of our people who decided to try and duplicate the "talking leaves" of the white man. He was a skilled silversmith, but had suffered an injury that left him lame. He studied our language and found that we had eighty-six separate and distinct sounds. He started writing down symbols for each of the sounds. Using the English alphabet for symbols, he quickly ran out of letters to use.

His people made fun of him and told him he couldn't make the things of the white man. His wife was always after him to do some silverwork to help bring in food for the family. It was a very difficult time for him. One day, after he had been working on the symbols for several years, he was out of the cabin and his wife took everything he had been working on and threw it in the fireplace. He came home, saw what his wife had done and said, "Gosh darn it! I wish you hadn't done that!"

Since we don't have any curse words in our language he was very limited in what he could say. Once again, he started working with the symbols.

Finally the alphabet was finished. He took it to his tribal council and showed them that it worked. The council adopted his alphabet as the official written language of the Cherokee. The man's name was Sequoyah. If you spoke the Cherokee language, all you had to do was learn what symbol stood for what sound. In two to three weeks a person could read and write in Cherokee. It did not matter what came before the symbol or what came after; it was always pronounced the same. Because it is written, our language will never die out. Sequoyah could not read or write in any language. He took another culture's model and made it a reality for his people.

THE SMOKY MOUNTAINS

Before Selfishness came into the world a long time ago, the Cherokee were happy using the same hunting and fishing lands as their neighbors. But all this changed when Selfishness came into the world and men began to quarrel.

The first quarrel of the Cherokee was with a tribe from the east. Finally, the chiefs of the two tribes met in council to settle the quarrel. They smoked the pipe and quarreled for seven days and seven nights.

The Great Spirit was displeased because people are not supposed to smoke the pipe until they make peace. As He looked down on the old men sitting with their heads bowed, He decided to do something

to remind all people to smoke the pipe only when making peace.

The Great Spirit turned the old men into grayish flowers, which we now call "Indian Pipes," and made them grow wherever friends and relatives have quarreled. He made the smoke hang over the mountains until all people all over the world learn to live together in peace.

SPEARFINGER

We had monsters in our culture. Some of these were shape-shifters, or those who could change their shapes to look like anybody they wanted to. This shape-shifter looked like a little old lady in her normal shape. Her skin looked like regular skin, but it was as hard as stone. Arrows would hit her and bounce off; spears would hit her and break. She could change her entire shape except for her right index finger. This finger was a little longer than normal. This was how she got her name: "Spearfinger." She was a monster because she lived on human livers. She always kept her finger hidden with a robe over her right wrist, or a basket over her right wrist

and her finger hidden down in the basket so no one could see it.

If she could get close to people she would stab them with her finger and they would seem to go to sleep. She would open the bodies, take out the livers and cause the bodies to heal up. In a little while the people would wake up. They would feel no pain and wouldn't know what had happened. In a few days, they would take sick and die. Everyone would know that Spearfinger had taken their livers.

Spearfinger was always roaming the woods looking for her next meal. If she saw young people in the woods, she might say, "Come here little ones. I have some honey in this basket and you can eat it while I comb your hair." If the children had been properly trained by their parents not to talk to strangers in the woods, they would run away.

In the fall of the year, the Cherokee would burn the leaves off the mountains to get at the nuts underneath. When Spearfinger saw the smoke rising into the sky, she would know the Cherokee were out on the mountains and she had a chance for another meal. When someone went into the woods by himself, the others never knew if the person coming back was the same one or if it was Spearfinger who had taken his shape.

Spearfinger killed so many of the Cherokee that finally they held a great council. All of the Wise Men and Warriors met for days trying to figure out a way to stop Spearfinger. After a long while they came up with a plan they thought would work.

They made sure all the people stayed in their villages, and then the Warriors went far back into the mountains. They selected a path that led far back into the Great Smoky Mountains. They dug a deep pit and covered it with branches and leaves so it looked like a part of the path. They built a large fire by the side of the path and hid themselves in the bushes.

Spearfinger looked out of her lair from far back in the Great Smoky Mountains and saw the smoke. She started down the path, looking for another meal. She carried her basket over her right wrist.

Soon the Warriors heard someone coming down the path singing a song. Around a bend in the path came a little old woman with a basket over her right wrist. They quietly watched as she walked down the path and stepped out on the branches. The branches broke and dropped her into the pit. When Spearfinger hit the bottom of the pit, she jumped to her feet and started screeching and yelling and clawing at the side of the pit.

The Warriors quickly surrounded the pit and looked down on Spearfinger. When Spearfinger looked up and realized that it was the Cherokee who had tricked her, she became more enraged and clawed even harder at side of the pit. The Warriors realized she would be able to claw her way out of the pit in a short while. They started shooting arrows and throwing their spears down at her.

The arrows would bounce off and the spears would break when they hit her. Spearfinger laughed and told them what she would do to them when she got out of the pit. Then a little bird flew over the pit and sang a song that sounded like the Cherokee word for heart. They took this as a sign to aim at her heart. Again, the arrows bounced off and the spears broke.

They caught the bird and clipped his tongue. The Cherokee know this bird as a liar. When it sings near a home it doesn't mean a loved one is coming home. Then another bird flew down into the pit and landed on Spearfinger's right hand next to her index finger. They took this as a sign to aim at her right hand. When they did, they saw Spearfinger's face change from anger and rage to fear and terror because her heart was contained in the palm of her right hand and she always kept her right fist tightly closed to protect it.

Finally, an arrow struck her at the base of her index finger and she fell over dead. And that is the story of Spearfinger.

The Trail of Tears

In the late 1820s gold was discovered in north Georgia near a town called Dahlonega. At that time, the Cherokee were living in north Georgia. It was thought that there was more gold on Cherokee lands. The governor of Georgia was trying to get the Cherokee moved out of Georgia, and he asked the government in Washington for help. Andrew Jackson was president at the time. He signed into law the Indian Removal Act, which called for the removal of all of the Indians who lived east of the Mississippi to the West.

White settlers started moving onto Cherokee lands. They claimed the land for themselves and started charging Cherokee rent for their own land.

The Cherokee appealed to the state of Georgia for help and the governor refused to help them. They then turned to the Department of Justice in Washington for help. The U.S. Supreme Court Justice Marshall ruled that Georgia was wrong and that U.S. government troops should be sent in to help the Cherokee.

President Jackson refused. He said, "Justice Marshall has made his decision, now let him enforce it!" No U.S. troops were sent in.

The Cherokee refused to move to the West. The government in Washington sent in an Indian agent, whose specialty was getting treaties signed by Indian tribes. He was called Reverend Schermerhorn. His assignment was to get a treaty signed by the Cherokee agreeing to move to the West. He went among the Cherokee telling them that the Great White Father in Washington wanted to give them all of this level land west of the Big Muddy, which is what we called the Mississippi. They wouldn't have to try and farm the steep mountainsides anymore. They needed to come to a meeting at New Echota, Georgia, and sign a piece of paper to get their land.

The Cherokee leaders realized what Schermerhorn was trying to do. They went among their people telling them not go to this meeting. They tried to tell them that they didn't know what Schermerhorn was really trying to get them to do. But, as always, there was a small group of people who did not listen. This group went to the meeting and signed their names to the paper.

Schermerhorn immediately sent the paper to Washington. Cherokee Chief John Ross left for Washington also. He talked to everyone who would listen. He told them that the majority of his people did not sign this paper, that none of their major leaders had signed the paper and that it had been signed by only a handful of people who didn't know what they were signing.

But the paper was sent to the U.S. Senate and they voted to accept it as being signed by the Cherokee Nation by only one vote. When word reached the Cherokee that the treaty had been accepted, a group of Cherokee immediately left for Indian Territory in Oklahoma. The rest stayed where they were.

Six months passed, and then a year passed, and nothing happened. The Cherokee thought Washington had forgotten about them. Washington was still having trouble with Indians out West.

Then, in the spring of 1838, federal troops showed up in Cherokee country. They built stockades and then started rounding up the Cherokee. The troops learned that if they came in the early morning they could catch all of the family at home before they went out to do their chores. They moved so quickly that a father might have been milking the cow when the troops showed up and he would only have time to turn the cow out into the pasture and grab what he could carry in his hands. Then he and his family would be driven down the trail. Sometimes, before they were taken out of sight of their home, other whites would enter to ransack the house, drive the livestock out of the pasture and set fire to the house.

Many times the soldiers would use their bayonets to move the people down the trail. One small family had been rounded up and was moving down the trail. The family's leader was an old man named Tsali. His wife, Wiloni, was old and couldn't move very fast. The soldiers used their bayonets to keep her moving faster. The family spoke to each other in Cherokee, which the soldiers didn't understand. They decided that farther on down the trail, they would give a signal and then would jump the soldiers and take their weapons. Farther down the trail the signal was given and the family turned on the soldiers. In the struggle, one of the soldiers was shot and killed. Tsali and his family grabbed the soldier's weapons and fled into the mountains.

General Winfield Scott was responsible for moving the Cherokee out West. When he heard that a soldier had been killed by the Cherokee, he sent word to our tribal council, telling them that if Tsali and his family did not come in and give themselves up to be executed, all of the Cherokee who were hiding in the mountains would be shot on sight as "outlaws." The tribal council sent word to Tsali to come in.

Tsali brought his family in. His youngest son was taken aside because of his age. The rest of his family was lined up and the soldiers lined up Cherokee warriors opposite them. Soldiers put weapons in the hands of the warriors and they were forced to shoot Tsali and his family. This was to show the Cherokee that they could not stand against the might of the U.S. government. The removal of the Cherokee had begun.

Our elders realized they would never see their beloved homelands again, and some of them just lay down and died. The family would move off to the side and dig a shallow grave as best they could with their hands and sharpened sticks. They would then pile stones high on top of the grave. This would protect it from animals and make it easier to find. They hoped one day to come back, find the grave and put a proper marker on it.

In the heat of that summer, and the snow and ice of that winter, four thousand of my people—nearly a quarter of the entire Cherokee Nation—died and were buried in nameless graves. We call it the "Trail Where They Cried."

You know it as the "Trail of Tears."

Why the Turkey Gobbles

Now, the Turkey had heard the Grouse give his good yell in the ballgame, and the Turkey wanted to have a good yell like the Grouse. So he went to the Grouse and asked the Grouse to teach him how to yell.

The Grouse agreed, but he said, "You have to give me something if you want me to teach you."

Turkey said, "Well, what do you want?"

And the Grouse said, "Give me some of your feathers."

Turkey gave him some feathers, and the Grouse put them around his neck, and then he started teaching the Turkey his yell.

Every morning they would get together and practice the Turkey's yell. Finally, the Turkey felt that he was ready. So, the Grouse went through the valley telling all the animals to listen the next morning. Early the next morning, the Turkey and the Grouse went up on a ridge. The Grouse jumped up on a hollow log and beat his wings against it to get everybody's attention. Then, Turkey jumped up on the log, cleared his throat and took a deep breath. He was so excited because he knew that everybody was listening.

But he couldn't yell, and all that came out was, "Gobble, gobble, gobble."

That's why the Turkey gobbles. The Grouse kept the Turkey's feathers and they form a ring around his neck to this day.

WHY THE TERRAPIN'S SHELL IS CRACKED

The Possum and the Terrapin met to hunt for food. They went through the forest searching for food. They found a persimmon tree that was heavy with fruit. The Possum climbed the tree to reach the fruit. Then the Possum selected a fruit for himself and tossed another down to the waiting Terrapin. After a while the Possum would not even look down when he dropped the fruit. He knew the Terrapin would take his time getting to the fruit on the ground. The Terrapin would always thank him for dropping the fruit down to him.

Then Possum realized he hadn't heard Terrapin thank him for a while. He looked down and there was a big Wolf standing over the Terrapin. When Possum pulled off another fruit and dropped it, the Wolf quickly grabbed it before it hit the ground. He would then stand over Terrapin and wait for another. Terrapin was not saying anything because the big Wolf could crush his shell with his jaws.

Possum moved to another branch as he thought how he could help Terrapin. He grabbed another fruit and dropped it. The Wolf dashed over and snatched it out of the air. Possum now knew what he would do. He kept dropping fruit as he searched the tree. Finally, he saw a large green persimmon. He pulled it loose and dropped it. The Wolf dashed over and snatched this out of the air also, but this green one was too large and lodged in his throat. The Wolf tried to dislodge the persimmon but he had been too greedy and tried to swallow before he realized how large it was. The persimmon choked the Wolf to death.

The Terrapin waited until he was sure the Wolf was dead. Then he took out his knife and cut off the Wolf's ears. He dried and shaped them so he could use them as spoons. He put a hole in them, ran a thong through the hole and put the thong around his neck. That was how he carried the wolf's ears around with him.

It was the custom among the people in those days to put gruel out beside the door for anyone to eat if they were hungry. The Terrapin came to a home and decided to eat. He used the Wolf's ear as a spoon. People saw this and started talking. The Terrapin had killed a Wolf! The Terrapin continued on and soon he came to another home. Word had spread faster then the Terrapin could walk.

These people had heard the story and wanted to see for themselves if it was true, so they invited the Terrapin to eat. He took the ears from around his neck and used them once more as a spoon. The people watched in amazement. It was true! Word was spreading before the Terrapin had finished eating. In a little while, Terrapin was full. He thanked the people and started on his way.

By this time, word had reached the Wolves. They called the pack together with their howls. When all of the pack had gathered, they were told what had happened. They all set out through the forest to seek revenge on the Terrapin for killing a member of their pack.

The Terrapin knew when he heard the howling that the pack was gathering to seek revenge on him. He started out as fast as he could go to find safety. It wasn't long before the Wolves picked up his trail.

Their howls were not far away. The Terrapin came to the edge of a high cliff with a river far below. He could hear the Wolves rushing through the forest. As the Wolves burst out of the forest they saw the Terrapin and their snarls made his blood run cold. They would tear him to pieces! He had to choose: wait for the Wolves to tear him apart or take his chances with the cliff.

Terrapin jumped off the edge of the cliff. The Wolves dashed to the edge of the cliff and watched silently as the Terrapin fell into the river. The impact was so great that the Terrapin's shell was broken into many pieces. As the Terrapin sank under the waters, he sang a medicine song that pulled his shell back together and mended it. He sank to the bottom of the river and started walking. He slowly walked out of the river on the other side. His shell showed where it had been pulled back together and healed. You can still see where it was healed to this day.

Uktena

The Cherokee fought many battles with the Shawano. In one battle, they caught a great Shawano medicine man. His name was "the Groundhog's mother." The Cherokee tied him up and were getting ready to torture him. The Shawano begged for his life and told the Cherokee that if they would spare his life, he would get the great crystal of the Uktena.

The crystal was in the forehead of the great Uktena serpent. If a medicine man could get the crystal, it would make him the greatest medicine man ever known. But to meet the Uktena meant that the person would die. The Cherokee told the Shawano about this. He laughed and said that he

was not afraid. His medicine was strong! They told him they would spare his life if he would bring back the crystal. The Shawano quickly agreed.

The Uktena was a great serpent and would wait in ambush in remote and hidden places. Uktena had learned that the Cherokee would use the mountain gaps to travel from valley to valley. He would select the darkest gaps with many places to hide and he would wait for them there. The Cherokee told the Shawano about the Uktena's ambushes.

The Shawano went to the northern border of Cherokee country. There, he found a great Blacksnake that was larger than any that had ever been seen before. He said, "Hah! You are too small!" And he continued searching.

He went to another gap, and there he found a great Moccasin Snake—the largest anyone had seen. But when people asked him about it later, he said it had been too small to notice.

At another gap he found a Green Snake, and he called the people to come see the pretty Green Snake. When they got to the gap, they saw a huge Green Snake with coils that overflowed the gap. They ran away in terror.

At another gap he found a great Lizard, but it was not what he wanted so he paid it no attention.

He traveled south, and at the Frog Place he found a great Frog sitting in the gap. When the people came to see it, again they ran away in terror. He laughed at them for running away from a Frog and continued on.

At other places he found great monsters of all kinds, but they were not what he was looking for and he continued searching. He went to the Leech Place on the Hiwassee and thought that the Uktena might be hiding in the deep pool. He dived into the waters and great Fish would rush at him and turn away. He saw many other monsters under the water, but they were not what he was looking for so he came out of the water and continued to the south. Finally, he found the Uktena asleep on a mountain.

Quietly, he took a deep breath and silently ran down the side of the mountain as far as he could go on the one breath. When he stopped, he made a big circle of pine cones. Inside of this circle, he dug a trench. He set fire to the pine cones and went back up the mountain.

The Uktena was still asleep when he returned. He drew back his arrow and sent it flying into the seventh spot back from the Uktena's giant head. This is where the Uktena's heart is located. The Uktena looked around and saw the Shawano running down the mountain. Uktena started after him, the crystal in his forehead flashing. The Shawano ran down the mountainside, jumped over the burning pine cones and cleared the trench. He quickly lay down inside the circle of fire. The Uktena didn't get far; the arrow had pierced his heart and he was dying. He threw his coils around, spitting his poison all over the mountain.

The poison couldn't get past the circle of fire—it would hiss and sputter as it hit the fire. But one small drop got inside the circle and hit the Shawano in the forehead. He didn't know it had landed on him. The Uktena's blood was pouring from its wound. The blood was also poisonous and flowed down the mountain. The trench stopped the blood before it got to the Shawano and he was safe. In its dying struggles, the Uktena knocked down trees and flattened bushes all around him. Slowly, it rolled down the mountain until it came to rest at the bottom. The Shawano called in all of the Birds to feast on the Uktena, and then he left. The Birds ate everything.

Seven days passed before the Shawano returned to the place where the Uktena had died. He came at night. The Birds had cleaned everything up. As he looked around, he saw something sparkling in the bushes. He went over to it. It was the great crystal of the Uktena. He knew the crystal would make him the greatest medicine man the tribes had ever known. He wrapped it up and took it with him.

As he traveled back to the village, he met many people. They all had heard of his travels and were anxious to hear of his adventures. When they saw him, they all were astonished. Where the small drop of the Uktena's poison had landed on his forehead a small snake was now hanging. The people never told him about it. As long as he lived, he never knew the snake was there.

WOUNDED KNEE

In the late 1800s, Indian tribes across the United States had been gathered together on reservations. For a people who were used to traveling where they wanted, when they wanted, for as long as they wanted this caused a lot of anger. They were told, "You will live on this piece of land and when you want something to eat, you will go see the Indian agent and he will give you something to eat." Many times they had never eaten the type of food they got from the Indian agent. There was a lot of anger and resentment among the tribes.

Then, one day, a Paiute holy man named Wovoka had a vision. When he awoke, he called his people together. He told them he had been shown that if they did a special dance, the Buffalo would come back, the white man would disappear and all those who had died from the bullets and disease of the white man would come back again.

He taught his people the dance, and soon other tribes heard of the dance. They would send people from their reservations to learn the dance and bring it back to their people. The dance spread from reservation to reservation. Finally, it reached the Lakota reservations. Shirts were made to use in the dance. It was said that they were medicine shirts and had the power to turn aside the bullets of the white man and send them across the plains where they would not hurt anybody. The dance was known as the Ghost Dance and the shirts were known as Ghost Dance Shirts.

The army informed the government in Washington, D.C., about the Ghost Dance. When the men in Washington heard about all of the tribes doing the dance, they thought this was the beginning of an Indian uprising on a massive scale. They sent word back to the army to make lists of tribes who were supporting the dance and ordered it to stop the dancers by any means necessary.

Sitting Bull of the Hunkpapa Lakota had supported the dance. Indian police came to arrest him. His followers resisted, and in the ensuing fight Sitting Bull was killed by the Indian police. Fearing the anger of the army, many of his followers fled to Sitting Bull's half brother, Big Foot, for protection. Big Foot led a small band of Minconjou Lakota. When he heard that Sitting Bull had been killed by the Indian police, he feared for his small band, for he too had supported the Ghost Dance. He found out that his name was on the army's list. He decided to take his small band to Red Cloud's reservation for protection.

It was the middle of winter and Big Foot was sick with pneumonia. He was so weak he couldn't sit on a horse. His people put him in the back of an open wagon and they left for Red Cloud's reservation.

The Seventh Calvary had been reformed after its disastrous defeat at Little Big Horn many years before. They were in charge of making sure the Minconjou stayed on their reservation. When they found out the Minconjou had left, a group of soldiers set out after them. It wasn't long before some of Big Foot's scouts came up to tell him that the soldiers were approaching quickly. Big Foot had a white flag raised on his wagon to show the soldiers that they didn't intend to fight. The soldiers caught up with Big Foot and the soldier's scouts said there were too many Lakota. They advised that it would be better to wait until the rest of the troop caught up with them the next morning before trying to collect the Minconjou weapons.

That night the Minconjou camped in a valley surrounded on three sides by ridges. Soldiers were stationed on two ridges with the valley in the middle. They had two Hotchkiss cannon that they placed on the third ridge. The cannon were facing down the row of lodges of the Minconjou.

The next morning the rest of the cavalry caught up with them. They brought with them two more cannon. These were placed on the ridge with the other two. Soldiers went down into the camp. They counted about 350 Lakota, most of them women, children and old men. They told the warriors to bring out their weapons. The warriors brought out bows and arrows, spears and tomahawks.

The soldiers were not satisfied. They started going into the lodges and found more weapons. Suddenly, an officer was struggling with a warrior who had hidden a rifle under his robe. A shot rang out and the officer fell to the ground. The soldiers on the ridges started firing down into the camp. The four cannon started shooting into the camp. Warriors were struggling with the soldiers and trying to get to their weapons so they could fight back. A large group of women and children started running toward a nearby gulch to get away from the fighting. Several soldiers saw them running and turned their horses after them, shooting at them as they ran. The soldiers killed them all.

The shooting was so constant, a survivor said, that "it sounded like someone was slowly tearing a large piece of canvas." When the shooting finally stopped, over 150 Lakota men, women and children lay dead and 25 soldiers had been killed, many by their fellow soldiers. A blizzard was moving in, so the dead Lakota were left where they had fallen and the wounded were loaded into wagons and taken to a nearby army post. At the post, they did not know where to put the wounded so they were left in the wagons in the freezing temperatures of the blizzard while a decision was made. Finally, a small chapel was cleared out and straw was thrown on the floor. The wounded Lakota were laid down on the straw.

Black Elk, a Lakota holy man, walked among the bodies that day. Later, in his old age, he would talk about that day:

> *When I look back now from this high hill of my old age, I can still see the butchered women and children*

lying heaped and scattered all along that crooked gulch, as plain as the day I saw them with eyes still young. And I saw that something else died there in the bloody mud and lay buried in the blizzard. A people's dream died there. It was a beautiful dream. And I, to whom so great a vision was given in his youth, you see me now, a pitiful old man who has done nothing. For the sacred hoop is broken and scattered, there is no center any longer and the sacred tree is dead.

The date was December 29, 1890. The place was called Wounded Knee.